Special thanks to:

My mother, Beatrice Elizabeth Bridges, for everything; my children and family for their continued encouragement; and all praise to the Most High for giving me a dream and the direction to bring it to fruition.

"Keep the Peace: Youth Writing Compilation and Interactive Workbook"

In Spirit Power and Truth Publishing, LLC
Columbus, OH

No part of this publication may be reproduced in whole or in part, or stored in a retrieval system, or transmitted in any form or by any means, electronic, mechanical, photocopying, recording, or otherwise, without written permission of the publisher and the copyright owners.

Copyright © 2017 Stephanie R. Bridges

All rights reserved.

ISBN-10: 1546882030
ISBN-13: 978-1546882039

For Carolyn Berkley

Contributors:

Ayanna Niambi, "Keep the Peace" Artistic Director, shared her creative talent and tireless work ethic to bring this book to fruition; Cynthia K. Price of Moving-Forward Communication, LLC, provided leadership during our workshops; and her time, energy and tangible content was instrumental to this publication; Derrick C. Lewis of Men of Courage provided the tap on the shoulder to bring this project to fruition, and I am inspired by his overall vision for our youth; The United Way has demonstrated their belief in our children and their potential for greatness with necessary resources; and a special thank you goes to A+ Arts Academy Staff and Students for their hospitality and participation.

Editor's Note:

This artistic collaborative creation was definitely a journey with mountains high and rivers wide; but no valleys low to speak of. When I had the bright idea to write a book with the young ladies at A+ Arts Academy, I didn't fully realize what I was getting myself into. What I thought would be a three month journey, turned into a three week end of school jaunt replete with absences due to testing dates, field trips, field day, out of state stays, and one young lady who took on the daily responsibility of letting me know she and a few others just weren't coming. Suffice it to say, there was not an opportunity for the twelve and thirteen-year-olds to draft, revise and edit their thoughts regarding peace.

What started as a series of lesson plans to enlighten youth, instill hope, and cultivate communal well-doing, shifted quickly into a series of checklists; photo, bio, release form, writing submission, painting, nametag. CHECK! But it was the writing that gave me pause. I do have a degree in Secondary English Education. I am a published author. Should I reach out to the parents and have them re-do, re-write, revise their offerings? Even though, I only attended school for the last three weeks of the school year, I deserved a break too. So, I put the middle school folder out of sight and out of mind.

Come crunch time, there was a last ditch effort over the summer break at A+ Arts Academy to add some polish to the work, and another last ditch effort at the main library to add some checks to the list. But more than anything, I got new young ladies; elementary school, high school, college age, and good and grown that provided more writing submissions for me to ponder. Hmmmm? Then it hit me – what if I published what they wrote? Their raw, uninhibited thought, without my judgement or redirection.

Now, there is very little in this book verbatim, but there is a lot of honest, young people expression. As an educator, I learned a long time ago, I get the pleasure of learning more from my students than I could ever teach. So, I won't mention any particular submissions; I'll just leave you with the opportunity to read with an open mind and learn. Yes, become enlightened, instilled with hope, and cultivated in communal well-doing by young people; the best people on earth. Peace.

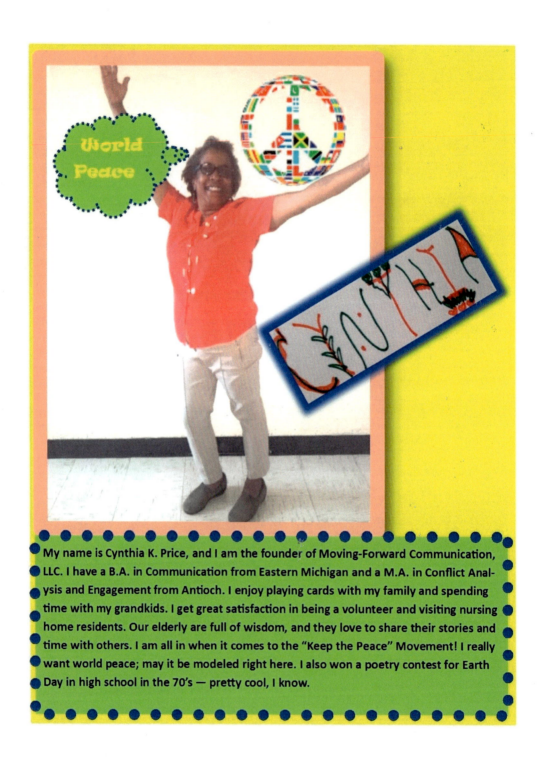

My name is Cynthia K. Price, and I am the founder of Moving-Forward Communication, LLC. I have a B.A. in Communication from Eastern Michigan and a M.A. in Conflict Analysis and Engagement from Antioch. I enjoy playing cards with my family and spending time with my grandkids. I get great satisfaction in being a volunteer and visiting nursing home residents. Our elderly are full of wisdom, and they love to share their stories and time with others. I am all in when it comes to the "Keep the Peace" Movement! I really want world peace; may it be modeled right here. I also won a poetry contest for Earth Day in high school in the 70's — pretty cool, I know.

"I define joy as a sustained sense of well-being and internal peace — a connection to what matters."

-Oprah Winfrey

Peace!
by Cynthia K. Price

Where is it?
Who has seen it?
Does it show up all blustery like a Chicago wind
or is it a cool island breeze,
doing its own thing?
Does it come by invitation only?
Or, does it sometimes just show up
at your door to sit and chat for a while?
Can it be cultivated like a prizewinning rose
or must you just wrestle with it?
Is it in our hearts
or, is it in our heads?
Can we feel peace
smell peace
taste peace.
Can we market peace?
What if we made a movie about it?
Can we buy it in a store or online?
Can we get it from Oprah –
you're getting peace, you're getting peace,
everybody is getting peace!

Anybody can have peace,
when they want it more than anything.

Questions:

Have you ever searched for peace? Where did you look? Who did you ask? Did you find it or, are you still searching for peace?

What is your Peace?

Kiarra R.

My name is Kiarra Roundtree, and I am currently a student at The Ohio State University studying Art Education. I also have a B.A. in Advertisement and Graphic Design from Columbus College of Art and Design. Creating has always been my passion! In my free time, I maintain my slight obsession with tea, my growing mug collection, and I enjoy photography by snapping all the interesting places and cuisine I come across. I am truly fond of the "Keep the Peace" Movement because it displays the individuality of others who all have their own unique interpretation of Peace. I am honored to be a part of this movement, and I cannot wait to show others what I have to bring to the table!

"I consider myself a crayon. I may not be your favorite color, but one day you are going to need me to complete your picture."

-Lauryn Hill

A Peaceful Statement
by Kiarra Roundtree

When I think of peace, I think of unity; when all people come together with no judgement. Unity can happen, if we depict each other based on our character and not our characteristics. When I see a world that behaves like this, that's when we are truly a peaceful human race. For our children, our future children, and generations to come, I advocate that this day will actually come to pass and no longer be only a dream of mine. I will display love, peace and unity in my future art and work with children, so I can show others how I wish to see the world. Maybe, one day, the "Keep the Peace" Movement will advance toward being universal.

Questions:

What comes to mind when you think of peace? How do you demonstrate peace in your daily life?

It Starts with ME!

Aniya Estridge

My name is Aniya Estridge, and I am a freshman at East High School. I play volleyball for the East High Tigers, and I am a dancer. My dance team has won a lot of trophies. I like to travel for dance competitions and with my family to explore new places. One of my favorite places to go is Virginia Beach. I also enjoyed our trip to Washington D.C. I am not sure about the "Keep the Peace" Movement. When I get older, I want to be a model, because I love dressing up, and I'm pretty tall for my age. I have a gap in my front teeth, and that makes me unique. I also have a super cool dog name Rex!

Deal with yourself as an individual, worthy of respect and make everyone else deal with you the same way.

-Nikki Giovanni

Step Out on Faith
by Aniya Estridge

It was a nice sunny day. Sarah and I had just gotten out of school, and on our way home, I saw him standing right there on the porch, only two houses down from mine. I wanted to introduce myself, but I was scared that he would make fun of my clothes. So, I ran home, leaving Sarah wondering what just happened.

I forcefully pushed opened the door and once I reached the top of the stairs, I called out, "Mom. Have you seen my jewelry?"

My mom opened her bedroom door and began matter-of-factly, "Of course, Ebony, it is in the same place I always keep it, but it is only for special occasions. You know that."

"Well, I need it now!" I exclaimed, still out of breath.

"For?" She asked with furrowed brow.

I blurted out, "These clothes…and the neighbor…Sarah has the…" My words could not match the speed of my thoughts.

Mom inhaled deeply, and looked into my eyes as she spoke, "I get that you hate your clothes, but that is all we can afford. Not everyone has the same amount of money to budget on clothes and shoes. All that stuff is temporary, anyway. Your jewelry is an heirloom from Grandma. You don't need to impress some guy or girl to be your friend."

Before I could reply, there was a knock on the door. I bounded back down the stairs and looked through the peep hole. I turned and my mom was standing at the top of the steps, "Thanks, Mom, for everything." I said with a sheepish grin.

I opened the front door. "Hey, what happened, Ebony?" Sarah asked.

"Oh, thaaaat…", I began with a giggle, as I stepped out to hang out with Sarah and the new neighbor.

Questions:

Have you ever been too embarrassed to talk to someone? If so, why? Do you have someone you can talk to when you feel this way?

My name is Miyah Evans, and I attend A+ Arts Academy. My favorite thing to do is go swimming. I am on a dance team, and we won 1st place in a competition. I enjoy doing people's hair. So, I would like to become a cosmetologist. I like to travel. Every February, I go to Alabama for my Grandfather's Pastor Anniversary. When I was a baby, I was in the hospital. It took a while for the doctors to figure out what was wrong. Because of that, my teeth are slightly discolored in the front, and I sometimes get teased. I like the "Keep the Peace" Movement because it inspires people to be better. I hope it will help end bullying at my school. Oh, and I like collecting coins!

"What's right isn't always popular, and what's popular Isn't always right."
              -Sharon Draper

Choices
by Miyah Evans

My name is Miyah. I am 11 years old and in the 6th grade. I go to A+ Academy. This is about my life story:

I usually hang out with people who are positive and have good grades. But sometimes I don't do that, and it gets me in trouble. I hang around people who are popular, but they bully others. Then I get in trouble for trying to fit in with the wrong crowd. A few weeks ago, I was in the dance room, dancing. Then all of a sudden, I got caught up in some mess that I did not want to be in. A storm of people were bullying *me* in one way or another. I turned to who I thought was my best friend, and she was talking about me too. So, when the storm cleared and everybody else stopped, she was the only one *still* talking about me.

My name is Miyah, and I am trying to make better choices. I will no longer hang out with bullies, no matter how "popular" they are.

Questions:

Do you make smart choices at home, school and work? Do you have any friends who are bullies? Is it more important to be popular or to be nice?

No Justice No Peace

My name is Maliyah Jackson, and I attend A+ Arts Academy. I love playing sports; basketball, soccer, kickball and boxing; I box with my uncle. Gym is one of my favorite classes because I enjoy doing physical activity. I want to be a lawyer, when I grow up because they make a lot of money, and I want to be rich – very very very rich! The "Keep the Peace" Movement is fun, cool, awesome and exciting. It is designed to keep the peace; no more bullies. I like to spend time at my Grandma's house and travel with my family. My dad has two dogs. I also like putting hot sauce on my potato chips – yum!

You don't have to like everybody, but you have to love everybody.
                                             -Fanny Lou Hammer

Stuff that Helps You Remain at Peace

by Maliyah Jackson

1. Exercising
2. Racing
3. Swinging on a swing
4. Dancing
5. Sleeping
6. Jumping
7. Painting
8. Doing Art
9. Being in a competition
10. Watching YouTube
11. Stretching
12. Flipping
13. Doing a handstand
14. Doing a backbend
15. Humming
16. Walking in circles

Questions:

Do you do any of the activities on this list? Which ones help you remain at peace?

Tracey

It's time for Peace!

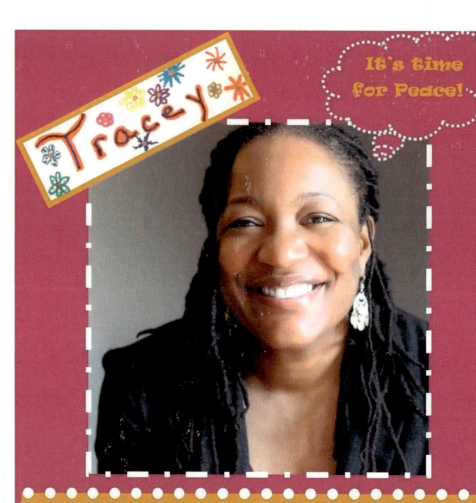

My name is Tracey Johnson, and I have a B.A. in Political Science from The Ohio State University. I am a Family Enrichment Center Manager, and my job literally entails helping people on their journey to improving their lives! When I'm not enjoying the best job ever, I like spending time with friends and family. I have three children, and three grandchildren. I believe the "Keep the Peace" Movement is incredibly timely. Because our society isn't always the most peaceful, learning tools to foster peace with one another and within ourselves could be far-reaching. Peace is imperative to a healthy society and psychologically healthy citizens. I'm also super obsessed with fishing. I can't get enough! I love the adrenaline rush of reeling in a fish.

"I had no idea history was being made. I was just tired of giving up."

-Rosa Parks

Fishing for Peace
by Tracey Johnson

If I'm to have peace with others, inner peace is a must. When I'm out of sorts, irritated, or disappointed with my own choices, I have a tendency to be less patient, more disagreeable, and quicker to anger with others. So, I have a variety of things that I do to help me find my own center – my inner peace. Those things have changed and evolved over time. That makes sense, because my interests have evolved as I've gotten older. What's most important to me now is that my tools for inner-peace are healthy.

With my interest changing over time, one thing has remained the same. Going fishing is a passion that hasn't changed, since my childhood. Fishing brings me a peace like nothing else can. Most people either like fishing, or they just don't get the big deal. I've found myself explaining a fishing trip with every detail and adjective I can muster, only to come to consciousness, look at the person's expression, and see they are baffled by my enthusiasm.

For me, there is nothing like fishing. First, there is being surrounded by nature. Getting away from the cement, buildings, crowds, traffic noises, and everyday sounds that come with populated areas. It's hard for me to settle my spirit with constant noise and commotion. Going fishing you can surround yourself with trees, an endless variety of plants, the sky and clouds, the smell of the outdoors, the diversity of wildlife, and the *water*!

Meditating on the waves, ripples and a leaf floating across the surface of the water brings me a sense of solace. Nothing else dances like water, and the dance is never the same. Whether I'm fishing in a lake, stream, pond or ocean; I can lose myself in the wonders of creation. I can go to the water troubled and find my spirit lifted with each wave reaching the shore; with each cast of my pole out to sea.

I've had inner turmoil before reaching the water, then found a sweet temporary distraction, when I felt the tug of a fish on my pole. I still get excited each and every time, just as I did, when I was 9 years old, and a fish would be pulling on my line! What kind of fish is it? How big is it? Will it put up a good fight? Will I be able to reel it in without it escaping? As much as I appreciate the environment, when I'm dancing with a fish, even the outdoors disappear. There is just me, my pole, the fish, and the water.

Oh, and what victory when I catch a fish! It never gets old pulling the fish out of the water. Just like when I was a child, I can't help but to imagine living in the wild; totally dependent on what I caught; at one with nature; maybe the way things once were.

The thing about fishing is that once I leave the water and make it back to reality, whatever was disturbing my peace is likely going to still be there. But, within that span of time while fishing – I can find perspective. Taking in nature and appreciating creation helps you do that.

I can find temporary reprieve from my trouble. A tug on my line and reeling in a fish requires my full attention at that moment; I've got to get it in! All other concerns disappear. I can have a victory. Catching a fish regardless of type or size, and reeling it in is a victory. Finding time to mediate away from professional and personal concerns is a victory.

So, I keep my fishing pole, tackle box, and fishing chair in my trunk. Time doesn't always allow me to fish as much as I want. I have a number of responsibilities. But whenever I can, and especially when I feel my inner-peace waning, I know where to find some perspective, reprieve, and victory to foster my peace – at the water with pole in hand.

Questions:

How do you maintain inner peace? How does inner peace impact interactions with others?

ASHA

Use Your Voice.

My name is Asha Bridges, and I am a senior at the HBCU, Howard University. I am pursuing a B.A. in Psychology with a minor in Chemistry. I like to travel, attend concerts – Lauryn Hill, Rihanna, and Janet Jackson are my favorites so far, and I love to read! My favorite book is "Their Eyes Were Watching God" by Zora Neale Hurston. I like the "Keep the Peace" Movement, because it is a step toward making the world a better place. Sometimes, I am quiet and find it difficult to talk to people. But this is something I am working on – using my voice. No matter how you best express yourself through speaking, singing, writing, art, dance, etc., always remember to use your voice.

It seems that fighting is a game where everybody is the loser.
-Zora Neale Hurston

Unknown Author
by Asha Bridges

my name is,
lost between your thoughts and your mouth
somewhere jumbled up in all of your labels
my name does not matter

you already have an idea of me
a name for me

I've already been placed in a cardboard box
marked with permanent letters

and that is all of me

But it is hard to breathe here
hard to be free here
boxed in

i am boxed in
Making myself small enough to fit your narrative
Small enough not to be seen, or heard

Too small
Small enough to not recognize who i am
Small enough to believe that i am not enough

But i am done being small
I am more than enough

And my name
my name is Free

Questions:

Have you ever felt judged by others? Has anyone ever labeled you something without getting to know you? How can you free yourself from other people's perception?

Post Up for Peace!

Jayla

My name is Jayla Gant, and I attend A+ Arts Academy. I like to go to the fair, watch television, play outside, and spend time with my niece. I am also a cheerleader and on a dance team; I have won trophies for both. When I grow up, I want to be a doctor because I like to help sick people. I would make sure the patient is ok *before* they leave the hospital. During the summer months, I like to go swimming and travel. I have been to Washington D.C. and Las Vegas, Nevada. I feel good about the "Keep the Peace" Movement. I think there should be posters in the school hallways and handouts given to the students as reminders to keep the peace.

"As long as you keep a person down, some part of you has to be down there to hold him down, so it means you cannot soar as you otherwise might."
                              -Marian Anderson

How Can We Get Along?
by Jayla Gant

1. Say nice things to each other.
2. Don't say anything sarcastic.
3. When someone bullies you, tell them to stop.
4. If they don't stop bullying, tell the teacher.
5. Don't be rude behind a person's back.
6. Don't be rude in a person's face.
7. Share with each other.
8. Put up posters to stop bullying.
9. Hand out papers to stop bullying.
10. Tell people to stop bullying!

Questions:

How well do you get along with others? What are some other things we should or shouldn't say or do, when attempting to foster peace?

Kyleigh.p

Peace is Amazing!

My name is Kyleigh Price, and I attend Berwick Alternative School. I like to dance and do flips for fun. I used to be on a dance team called Luv 2 Dance. We won a lot of competitions, but it ended this year. When I grow up, I want to be a professional dancer because I love to dance! At school, I have gotten the Principal Leadership Award, and I have won candy for winning games in class. I think the "Keep the Peace" Movement is an amazing and intelligent idea. My mom has a baking business that I sometimes help with. When I get older, I am going to make cakepops, get rich and buy my own studio; so, I can dance of course.

"It isn't where you came from, its where you're going that counts."
                    -Ella Fitzgerald

Peace.
by Kyleigh Price

SOMETHING YOU NEED
That you don't really get

Peace is amazing
It's what a lot of people need
Also, what they want

But if we get peace, some people will take advantage
But I won't; it's just what I need
But if you don't, that is on you

Peace is what a lot of people need
So, if you are in the way, back up

PEACE.

Questions:

Do you need peace in your life? Why is it that some people don't want peace for others or themselves?

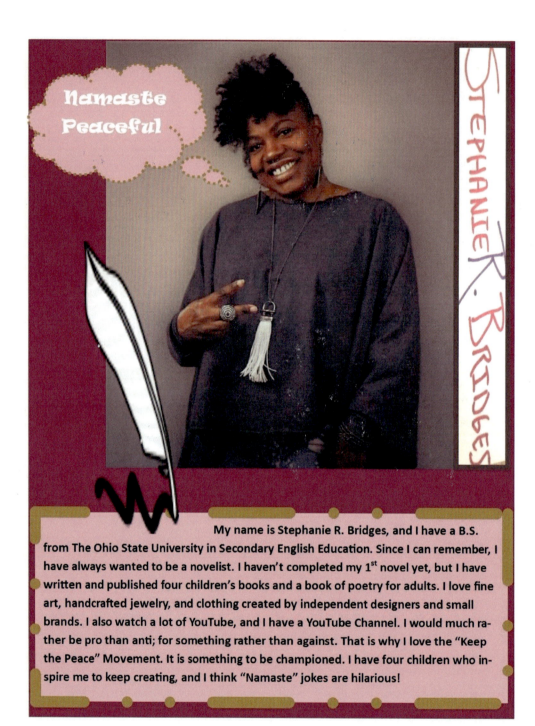

My name is Stephanie R. Bridges, and I have a B.S. from The Ohio State University in Secondary English Education. Since I can remember, I have always wanted to be a novelist. I haven't completed my 1st novel yet, but I have written and published four children's books and a book of poetry for adults. I love fine art, handcrafted jewelry, and clothing created by independent designers and small brands. I also watch a lot of YouTube, and I have a YouTube Channel. I would much rather be pro than anti; for something rather than against. That is why I love the "Keep the Peace" Movement. It is something to be championed. I have four children who inspire me to keep creating, and I think "Namaste" jokes are hilarious!

"I'm at peace with God and all mankind."
               -Harriet Tubman

5 Reasons I Love Me, and You Should Love You
by Stephanie R. Bridges

1. I Am the Closest Person to Me

No matter where I go, how far I travel, how much distance I put between myself and loved ones, I cannot escape me. Imagine if you are forced to be with another human being for the rest of your life, wouldn't you try to find some way to like them, even love them? For forty plus years of my life, I didn't give much thought to the relationship that I have with myself. I took it for granted. I disregarded the cornerstones that allow relationships to thrive – trust, communication, acceptance and encouragement. I continually work on all these facets with myself now. I **trust** that I have purpose, and I am on the right path. I am persistent in my effort to actualize all of who I am, because I trust my development and direction. I spend time **communicating** with me by meditating, writing, speaking positive affirmations and researching all aspects of my being. I **accept** all of me, and I celebrate every part; good, bad or indifferent. Through acceptance, I am able to make positive changes where necessary. Like Donald Lawrence and the Tri-City Singers told us, sometimes you have to **encourage** yourself. We all have goals, dreams and aspirations. When times are tough, sometimes an encouraging reminder from myself to myself is all it takes to keep making progress. Me, myself, and I are the coach, the star player and the head cheerleader. Rep your crew.

2. I Am a Masterpiece

Imagine you went to a museum and saw a painting. Let's say you weren't particularly moved by it, but you thought it was okay. Upon closer inspection, you realize it is an original Van Gogh. Now you cannot believe your eyes; it takes you a moment to catch your breath. You are standing in a room with a masterpiece. You are moved to alert everyone in your party about what you have discovered, and you spend the next few minutes staring in awe at what is clearly a one of a kind, original, priceless work of art; not because the painting has changed, but because you recognize the creator as a master. Well, I cannot believe my eyes. It takes me a moment to catch my breath, when I think about the depth and breadth of my greatness – not because I have changed, but because I finally recognize my Creator is the Master. I am moved to alert all to what I have discovered, and I invite you to stare in awe at the Master's Work. Just look in the mirror.

3. I Am Free

I stopped packing, labeling and delivering myself in a neat little conformist box based on what he, she and society say. I am free, liberated, created in the Image of God. I am a spirit; that is my true identity, everything else is made up. As long as, you identify with your core being, it doesn't matter how anyone else judges your flesh. I refuse to ever be subjugated to a race, gender, religion, nationality, you name it, again. Remember in school, when it is time to play a game, the teacher groups everybody by numbers. Everyone goes around the room and counts – 1, 2 ,3: 1, 2, 3: 1, 2, 3. All the 1's are on a team, all the 2's are on a team and so on. So, let's say that the 1's win the game and they are celebrating; the 2's come in 2nd place, and they are angry, because they feel like they were cheated; and the 3's come in last, and they are just ready for the bell to ring. But, once the game is over, everyone goes back to being an individual. Okay, the game is over! Oly oly in come free! You are no longer a number, statistic, or demographic. Stop playing a role that was handed to you, and start loving the authentic you. Yes, I still celebrate my heritage, spirituality, even my occupation, but that doesn't define me. It just reminds me no matter the score, I'm always on the winning team. Be the authentic you.

4. I Am the One and Only Me

When I would hear the statement - there is no one else quite like you - I took it to mean there is something special about my person, and there is. But I have come to realize - there is no one else quite like you - really means there is no one else that can do the things I can do. It is less about me being unique for the sake of self-celebration and more about me being unique for the sake of service. I have a purpose, and if I don't fulfill my purpose, I am letting down the universe. There are men, women and children waiting on me to do my thing, and I have been so caught up in my feelings that I almost stopped making it do what it do. What if Harriet Tubman, Nina Simone, or Michelle Obama had given up? Where would we be? Now take a moment and think of all of the people who actually have given up, even if it were only 10 greats in history. How much further could we be towards global conservation, space travel, medical breakthroughs, equal pay for women, global peace? I have a job to do. I am uniquely created for such a time as this, and so were you. I am waiting to hear your music, use your app, vote you into office, and celebrate your historical 1st.

5. I Am Here

For a long time, I looked for outward validation to gauge how I should feel about myself. This is a lose lose. When I didn't receive positive affirmation from parents, teachers, bosses, children, friends, etc., my esteem dipped, because I felt like I wasn't enough; I didn't measure up. When I did jump through all the necessary fiery hoops to be liked, appreciated and applauded my esteem dipped, because I lost sight of who I am and began to feel more like a show puppet rather than a person. Do people really like or even know me, or is it the way I look, the clothes I wear, my athleticism or humor? That is an excellent question, but first I had to learn to like me for me. I had to find my value in being, just being. It wasn't my accomplishments, talents, abilities or promotions. My birth is more than enough. I am excited about my existence. I am in awe of this instant. I relish my right now. I love me for me. Stop and take some time to acknowledge the wonder of your existence; the miraculous miracle that you are - period.

Questions:

Do you love yourself? What are some ways you can work on building a stronger relationship with yourself?

Don't just talk about it, be about it!

Pandora !!

My name is Pandora Brown, and I am a senior at the HBCU, Central State University. I made the Dean's List at my school, and I am a member of the NAACP – CSU Chapter. My primary goal is to become a talk show host of a program centered on encouraging, empowering, and uplifting young African Americans. I feel like the "Keep the Peace" Movement is important because people often talk about it, but very little is done. I smile and speak to everyone I encounter, because I don't know what that person may be going through. So, something as small as a smile and a hello, may have a positive impact on their situation. I love dancing and laughing with my friends.

"You've got to learn to leave the table when love's no longer being served."
-Nina Simone

R.E.S.P.E.C.T.
by Pandora Brown

Discovering peace within is key to giving and receiving respect. As a young woman, I had very little respect for myself. I was not really taught about it, and so it never really mattered to me. Things started to change, when I noticed my lack of self-respect impacted, not only how I treated people, but also how I allowed people to treat me. It also affected the level of peace I had within. When I decided to make a change in the level of respect I have for myself, I became a whole new woman. This has not only changed my view of the world, but the way I view relationships, as well. You cannot truly experience peace, until you find peace within. You can't give something you don't have. Once you increase the level of respect you have for yourself, you will become more at peace, and this sets the tone for how you interact with others.

Questions:

What does respect mean to you? Do you respect yourself? Do you show respect and expect respect from others?

Unity in the Community

My name is Tahleigha Burke, and I play volleyball and softball for East High School, where I am a senior. I earned the most improved varsity volleyball player, as well as the Ace Award. I am also in the Chess Club and in the Health Science program at my school. I have plans to become a doctor. I am all for the "Keep the Peace" Movement; I love the idea of keeping the peace in our community. I would like to see more originality and acceptance in schools, more overall happiness and less violence. On my down time, I like to go to local parks with my friends, and I love to travel with my family. I recently got a cute blonde terrier name Jinx.

"Take a deep breath. Pause"
-Iyanla Vanzant

Bloom Already
by Taleigha Burke

Everyone that I come across is perceived as a beautiful flower. Now, as cliché as it might sound, in my eyes it's 100% true. There are some who are late bloomers, and there are others who open up one petal at a time for those that pollinate them. Now, when I say late bloomers, I am not talking puberty! I'm talking about the introverts who are scared to let others in. The ones who are afraid to speak their opinions to the early bloomers, who they see basking colorfully in the sunlight. The late bloomers, afraid to be judged, remain in bud formation.

Many people in our society, this generation in particular, are not as accepting of those who are different. Even though, we would like others to be accepting of us. A flower or any plant for that matter needs nourishment - a little TLC (Tender Love and Care). You can't plant a seed in bad soil and expect it to turn into a beautiful rose. You will only get nasty weeds from that. Roses need water, pollen and sunshine.

We as a people, have neglected our introverts – our late bloomers. Society has become bad soil; storm clouds pouring down on the modest flower bed. "Speak up!", "We can't hear you!", "Say what's on your mind!", "Why are you so quiet?", "Don't talk to her. She's weird." Who will be the sunshine, when the flood comes? Even still, we must be careful what we allow to grace our rosebuds. Too much sunshine could bring a drought. There has to be a balance. Introverts need inclusion, acceptance *as is*, not an intervention to become something they're not.

Questions:

Are you an introvert or an extrovert? Do you have some qualities of both?

MaKayLa

Stop Bullying!

My name is Makayla Jackson, and I attend A+ Arts Academy. I like to run, play video games and sit on my front porch and watch YouTube. I love to do DIY projects on clothing, jewelry and art. In kindergarten, I had my artwork hung in a building downtown. Both of my grandmas have always made clothes, and they taught me. When I grow up, I want to continue my passion and become a clothing designer. I feel like the "Keep the Peace" Movement can change our school by helping to stop bullying, lessening suspensions and bettering grades. I once had a pet fish, and I also enjoy traveling. I've been to Tennessee, Florida, Georgia, Kentucky and Washington D.C., so far.

"What tried to demolish me, I allowed to polish me."

-India Arie

Just a Dreamer
by Makayla Jackson

Hey,
I'm just a dreamer thinking about the future
It is not always unicorns and rainbows
Sometimes it is weird things, good things, bad things, scary things
lots and lots of things
Most times, you don't know what your dream
is connected to…
Then there are my dreams
My scary, my weird dreams
Some are forgotten
Some always remain
Like the clock on my Grandma's night stand
Some so very fictional
Some so, so true
If you feel like I do, dreams are a simulator for you too
I remember lots of dreams
Like a limited-edition show
Unless there is a series of episodes…

Questions:

Do you feel at peace when you sleep? What do you dream about?

No More Bullying!

My name is Jahnyah Gussler, and I attend A+ Arts Academy. I enjoy playing basketball, and I have won trophies for the sport. I am also a girl scout, and I have received multiple badges for my efforts. When I get older, I want to be an administrative assistant because I love typing and talking on the phone. Sometimes when I get nervous, my legs shake. I have had a lot of pets over the years. I think the "Keep the Peace" Movement might be kind of good; I would like to see peace and no more bullying. During the summer, I like to go swimming and sometimes my mother takes me and my siblings camping. Every summer, we celebrate my birthday on June 22!

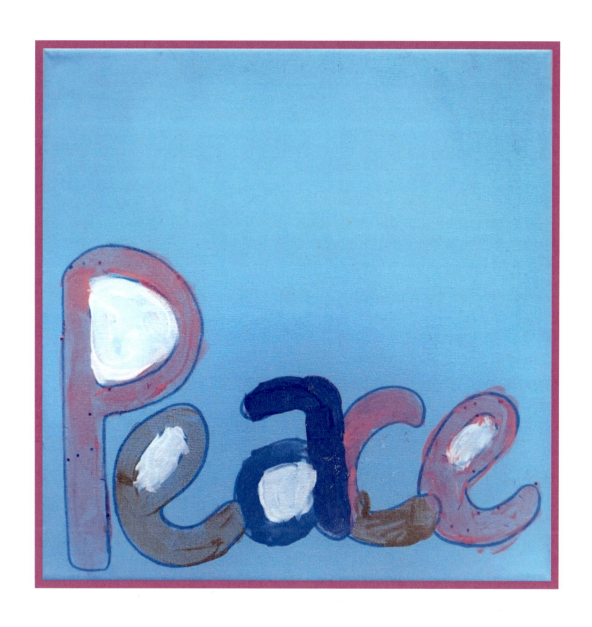

Hate is too great a burden to bear.
It injures the hater more than it
injures the hated."
                    —Coretta Scott King

There's a Lesson to be Learned
by Jahnyah Gussler

One day this girl was bullying
I told her to stop
Before she got popped
She looked at me like I was dumb
Then she put up one of her thumbs
I was like what does that mean?
She told me to shut up
So, then I had to run up
I punched her in the face
And she tripped over her lace
She said OMG! Look at that flea!
I'm like girl, I think it came off you, as I was still punching,
She said, I think it came off that tree
Then the girl that was getting bullied pulled me off
I told the one that got beat, she learned her lesson from a boss
What goes around comes around
Bullies jump up to get beat down
She stopped bullying forever
Okay, so then I got in the "Keep the Peace" Movement, and well…

I saw the girl that was bullying. I said, "Did you learn your lesson?" And I said, "*Sorry*. Next time I will handle it a different way." I asked her, "Do you want to be friends?"
She said, "Yeah."
"Okay, where is the girl that you were bullying?" I asked.
She said, "I don't know."
"Oh, there she is!" We both exclaimed in unison. We ran over and asked, "Do you want to be friends?"
She said, "Yes."
Then we all went to my house and played games and watched movies.

Questions:

Is fighting a good way to handle bullying? Why or why not?
What would you do if you saw someone else being bullied?

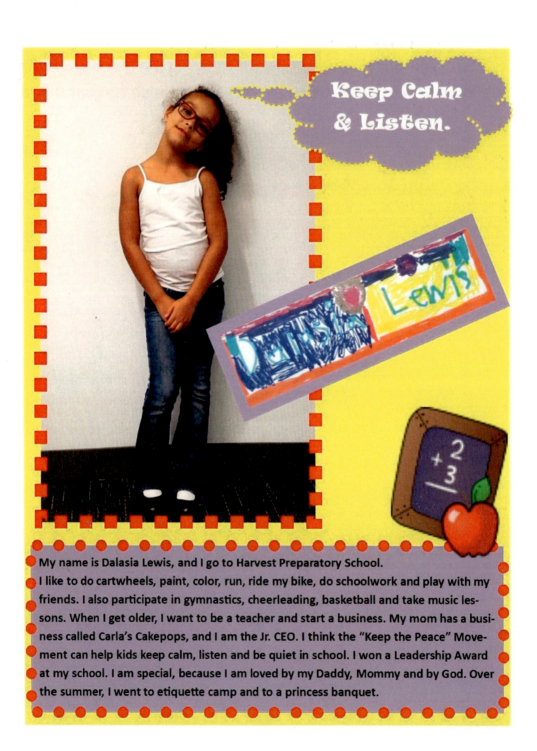

Keep Calm & Listen.

My name is Dalasia Lewis, and I go to Harvest Preparatory School. I like to do cartwheels, paint, color, run, ride my bike, do schoolwork and play with my friends. I also participate in gymnastics, cheerleading, basketball and take music lessons. When I get older, I want to be a teacher and start a business. My mom has a business called Carla's Cakepops, and I am the Jr. CEO. I think the "Keep the Peace" Movement can help kids keep calm, listen and be quiet in school. I won a Leadership Award at my school. I am special, because I am loved by my Daddy, Mommy and by God. Over the summer, I went to etiquette camp and to a princess banquet.

World peace and brotherhood are based on the common understanding of the contributions and cultures of all races and creeds.
-Mary McLeod Bethune

Time Out
by Dalasia Lewis

Today while I was out on the playground, standing by the green slide talking to my friend, London, a boy marched over to me, put his face close to mine and said, "I do not like you!" He then pushed me down.

The boy was a second grader, and he was bigger than me. I fell to the ground and hit my back and my head. Then I started crying. My friend, London, ran and told the teacher what happened. Then she came back and helped me up and walked with me to the nurse's office. I told the nurse what happened and she asked me, "On a scale from one to ten, how do you feel?"

I responded, "Pass ten to thirteen." I was happy that my friend stayed with me, but sad that I had gotten pushed down.

The nurse wiped my tear and said, "When you feel better you can go back outside." I'm glad that my friend London was with me the whole time.

We went back to the playground and all my friends came up to me at once and asked, "Where have you been; we were looking for you?" I told my friends that I had been in the nurse's office. It felt good that they were looking for me.

If I could say anything to the bully, I would say "I will not tolerate that!" But I couldn't, because he was in time out.

Questions:

Have you ever been bullied? How did it make you feel? Do you have friends who stand by you in tough situations?

My name is Adrienne G. Harris, and I have a B. S. of Education from Ashland College. I chose teaching as a career with encouragement from my mother. When I decided to drop out of school in 2nd grade, she said, "Try again tomorrow. Show them how it should be done." I enjoy doodling and distressing clothing to create DIY designs. I wrote a book; "What's in Your Heart? Seeing the Real Me", and I travel a great deal by plane and by train. I am excited to be a part of the "Keep the Peace" Movement; my heart is warmed by the smiles and comfort of others – that's just who I am. Wait, I almost forgot the bear that occasionally visits me; we call him the Garbage Can Bandit.

The moment anyone tries to demean or degrade you in any way, you have to know how great you are!

-Cicely Tyson

A Grade School Prayer:
by Adrienne G. Harris

Bless my endeavors throughout this day
Keep troubles, confusion and spiteful people far away
Away from my space, so that I've no need to fear
Lord, I desire peace, love, kindness, and respect to surround me

Yet and still, for some reason unknown by me
There are those who get their kicks in life
Out of kicking others around

Day after day, I think to myself:
If only she knew me, she wouldn't treat me this way
If only he knew me, he'd find something kind and polite to say

With repeated threats, I often pray:
Lord, if only for a few moments,
I wish to be invisible or just melt away
But why, Lord, should I disappear?

Please just stop their hands from inflicting pain
And freeze those nasty words in the very back of their throats

I believe, one day someone is going to rescue me
Oh yes, one of these days, just you wait and see
The loving kindness, compassion, understanding and care
You instilled within my heart will one day be noticed
Then those of a pure heart will finally see, the precious jewel,
The Real Me

Questions:

Why do you think some people are mean to others? Do you think people become nicer as they get older? Why or why not?

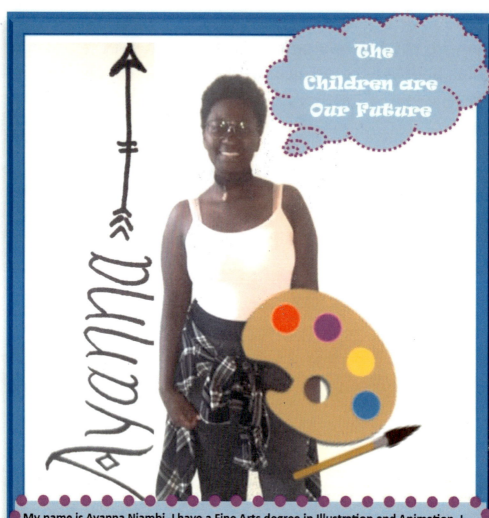

The Children are Our Future

My name is Ayanna Niambi. I have a Fine Arts degree in Illustration and Animation. I graduated Cum Laude from Columbus College of Art and Design with honors! I love taking walks, sketching outdoors, and spending time with family and friends. My focus right now is becoming a great artist, and maybe later, a writer as well. I illustrated the children's book, "My Favorite Color is Blue." I have a passion for books, music and creativity in all forms. The "Keep the Peace" Movement is truly a good thing; we need more positive influences for the youth, as they will impact the future. I am a child of God, and that alone makes me *very* special. Oh, and I like speaking with different accents – Russian is a frequent go-to.

"Peace will come wherever it is sincerely invited."

-Alice Walker

Just One of Those Days
by Ayanna Niambi

Imagine you're having what feels like the worst day ever! You wake up late, can't find your favorite pair of jeans, have to skip breakfast, and you still arrive late to school. How would you respond, if someone intentionally tried to tease, upset, or chastise you for seeming down? By this point, most would be aggravated and feel discouraged. They have no idea how you are really feeling. Now, place yourself in the shoes of someone else. It's important to remember that you don't really know how that person is feeling.

Often, people ask out of habit, "How are you?" or "How is your day going?" However, in most cases, no one really asks for the truth, and so we've become trained to respond with "good" or "fine." We should take care to ask others about their state of being out of love and care, not as small talk or a conversation-starter. Sometimes the only positive part of someone's day is when you sincerely ask about him or her, listen to what they have to say and give a supportive response. How would you want someone to treat you on your worst day? Give someone a hug, encourage others, keep the peace.

Questions:

Have you ever had a bad day? What happened to make it not so great? What happened to make it better?

My name is Nandi Bridges, and I attend Columbus Africentric High School. I am currently a junior, and I have been playing softball since my freshman year. I also attend Fort Hayes Career Center for half of the day and study Bio-Science Technology. After I graduate from high school, I want to attend an Historically Black College or University (HBCU). I currently have sisters at Howard and FAMU. My mother wrote a children's book about me called, "Can We All Just Get Along?" because I get along well with all my siblings. So, yes, I definitely agree with the "Keep the Peace" Movement. I also assist my mom with selling books at events. Everyone who knows me, knows I love shoes – I'm a sneaker head for sure.

"Unpersecuted, unjailed, unharrassed writers are trouble for the ignorant bully, the sly racist, and the predators feeding off the world's resources."
                                                            -Toni Morrison

You Might Just be a Bully:
Top 10 Things A Bully Might Say
by Nandi Bridges

10. "Everybody else was doing it too. I didn't start it."

9. "I was only joking/playing/kidding."

8. "I was just being honest. It's not my fault she is_____."

7. "She shouldn't be so sensitive. He's soft. Crybaby."

6. "I was just laughing. I was only telling her what they said."

5. "People talk about me too. Everybody gets teased."

4. "They dared me to do it. I just wanted to fit in."

3. "I didn't mean to hurt his feelings. It's just words."

2. "It was an accident. I didn't mean to trip/push/slap him."

1. "I just shared it online. I only showed it to one person."

Bonus

"I didn't mean for it to go this far. I wish I could take it back."

Questions:

Have you ever said any of these statements? Are these excuses for being a bully or justification for unintentional behavior?

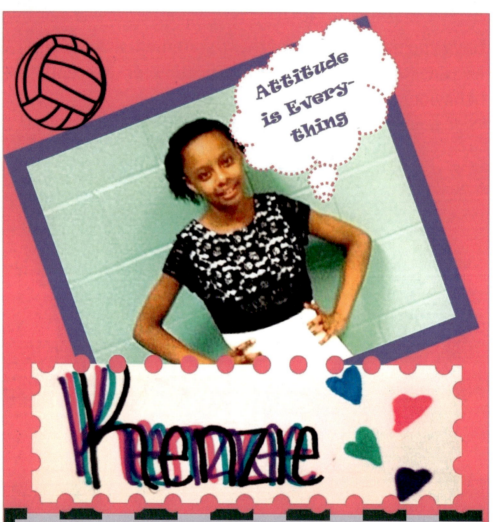

Attitude is Everything

Kenzie

My name is McKenzie Price, and I attend Berwick Alternative School. I enjoy dancing and playing volleyball for my school's team. I have won awards in school and trophies for dance competitions. During the summer, I attend camp, and I love to travel. This summer, I went to King's Island with my family. It was a lot of fun. I think the "Keep the Peace" Movement is very important, especially right now. I hope it can help the students' attitudes, and their relationships with teachers will improve. I don't know what I want to be when I grow up, but I do know—right now—I love to dance. I even have dance parties all by myself!

"When someone is cruel or acts like a bully, you don't stoop to their level. No, our motto is, when they go low, we go high."

-Michelle Obama

PEACE
By McKenzie Price

My eyes are useless
When the mind is blind
Making me unable to find
What's rightfully mine
PEACE

Where can I look
They said look inside
Where does it hide
I yelled and cried
PEACE

I dimmed the lighting
Closed my eyes
I felt it rise
I found my prize
PEACE

Questions:

Do you think everyone deserves peace? Why do you think some people have a harder time finding peace than others?

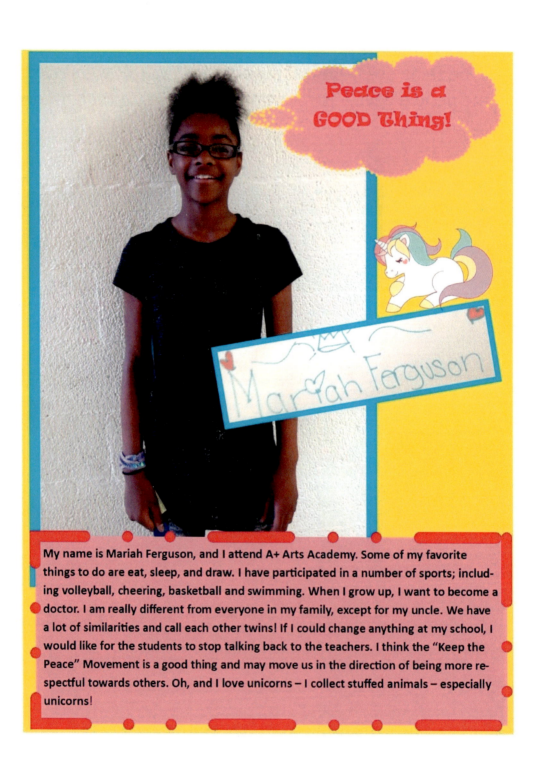

My name is Mariah Ferguson, and I attend A+ Arts Academy. Some of my favorite things to do are eat, sleep, and draw. I have participated in a number of sports; including volleyball, cheering, basketball and swimming. When I grow up, I want to become a doctor. I am really different from everyone in my family, except for my uncle. We have a lot of similarities and call each other twins! If I could change anything at my school, I would like for the students to stop talking back to the teachers. I think the "Keep the Peace" Movement is a good thing and may move us in the direction of being more respectful towards others. Oh, and I love unicorns – I collect stuffed animals – especially unicorns!

"I am no longer accepting the things I cannot change. I am changing the things I cannot accept."
-Angela Davis

 **Let Me Tell You a Story...**

by Mariah Ferguson

Once upon a time not long ago
I was 10 years old, wanted a rabbit and a troll
I was old enough to understand
How this life was going to end
But Jesus said, "Don't worry bout the end.
Jus' keep movin' like 2 pigs in a pen."
Now, I'm in the group "Keep the Peace" Movement
I think this might be Heaven Sent
We came up with a great idea
Bout taking the beginning
And making it the end of bullying
Let's 'Keep the Peace' and all be friends
And that's how this rap is going to end, end, end, end, end...

Questions:

Do you like to sing and rap? Can you write a song or rap about the "Keep the Peace" Movement?

"KEEP THE PEACE"
BY COLORING THE FOLLOWING PAGES

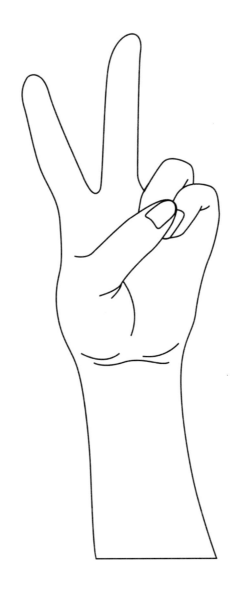

"KEEP THE PEACE" WORD SEARCH

```
L S Y T M Q Q A A C E U M B C
O W A S N U Z F I E A O N O T
V O G S R E L I E F T L M Q N
E O R E R R M E Q C O P M Y E
S S E N R E H T E G O T T R M
E A E I I F L P N S W I E O L
R H M P G N S A U E L S R B L
E G E P M E S R X I T D X P I
N E N A R A E M U A E N Q N F
I T T H E S D Q T R T C O P L
T S T I L L N E S S F I U C U
Y A O Y C A M O L P I D O R F
Z M L J R E C A E P Y O J N T
H A O T F R I E N D S H I P Q
Y N O M R A H U N I T Y F Q U
```

WORD LIST:

AGREEMENT
CALM
COMPOSURE
CONTENTMENT
DIPLOMACY
FRIENDSHIP
FULFILLMENT
HAPPINESS
HARMONY

JOY
LOVE
NAMASTE
ORDER
PEACE
RELAXATION
RELIEF
RESPECT
REST

SERENITY
STILLNESS
TOGETHERNESS
TRANQUILITY
TRUCE
UNITY
WOOSAH

FIND PEACE MAZE

PEACEFUL BREATHING

The next time you are worried, afraid or angry try this short breathing exercise. We can impact how we are feeling by changing and concentrating on our breathing.

1. **Sit or lie in a comfortable position.**
2. **Close your eyes.**
3. **Concentrate on inhaling and exhaling.**

Inhale and exhale through your nose. Your mouth should be closed with your tongue pressed against the roof. Relax your teeth and jaws.

4. **Become mindful of each inhale and each exhale.**

As you inhale, fill your lungs fully with air, let the breath flow all the way to your stomach. If you are laying down, put your hand on your stomach and feel it expand with air. Push all of the air out with the exhale as slowly as possible.

5. **After a few moments of working on deep inhales and slow exhales, begin to add these thoughts, coordinating with your breathing.**

Inhale Slowly: I breathe in peace.

Exhale Slowly: I breathe out love.

Repeat.

6. **As the exercise does its work and your tension begins to ease, take one final deep breath, exhale and then *smile*.**

AFFIRM YOUR PEACE

Step One:
Create an **Affirmation Board** with poster board and markers; a magnetized board and magnets; or a bulletin board and push pins.

Step Two:
Use markers to write directly on the board, or write on cardstock and add your words to your board with magnets or pushpins.

Step Three:
Write positive words **ONLY**. Do not use any words with mixed meanings or negative connotations. *Please ask parents and teachers for assistance.*

Step Four:
Say your affirmations daily –

I Am Peaceful	I Am Forgiving	I Am Thoughtful
I Am Caring	I Am Understanding	I Am Kind
I Am Friendly	I Am Joyous	I Am Gracious
I Am Non-Violent	I Am Calm	I Am Loving

PEACE IN A JAR

This jar is an artistic and kinetic monument to peace. Let me share the process. It was fun; you might enjoy it too.

Components:
1 water bottle
Uncooked rice, enough to fill up half your jar
A few drops food coloring
A little splash of vinegar
Various materials:
- Small rocks (The rocks represent obstacles. They are small because my monument is portable)
- Thyme seeds (This is a movement and seeds must still be planted. It will take time)
- Letter beads
- Heart beads
- Peace symbol beads
- Peace symbol stickers
- Jewelry making wire
- Gold cord
- Wire cutter
- Pencil

This is a two part process:

Part One -
Put approximately 2 cups of uncooked rice into a plastic storage bag
Add the food coloring and vinegar
Close the bag (Zip Locking the bag is important)
Knead until the color is thoroughly mixed into the rice
Spread the rice over a lined baking sheet to cure overnight

Part Two -
- Wash and dry the bottle
- Create word strings with the letter beads and wire
- First load the beads onto the wire while still attached to the spool. Start with the last letter and end with the first letter of the word. Make a curlicue on the end of the wire using a pencil; began cutting between the words subsequently curling each new end.
- Layer the components in the bottle:
    - Add a little rice
    - Add the rocks, the thyme seeds, and a little glitter
    - Add more rice
    - Add a few words
    - Then more rice
    - Then the peace and heart beads
    - More rice
    - The final words
    - More rice
    - And a lot of glitter
- Finally, cap the jar, add a sticker to the top and attach the cord, tying it in a bow.

Okay, now get ready to shake it up for PEACE!

JOURNAL FOR PEACE

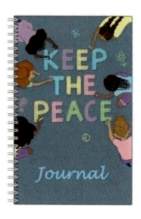

Journaling is an excellent way to release painful emotions and remind ourselves of positive experiences. You can use a journal, diary or notebook to write daily or weekly. Whenever you start a new journal, flip back to the last page and write a letter congratulating yourself on filling up your journal with thoughts, feelings, prayers and dreams. Journaling will also help improve your written communication skills and can be used for creative writing, as well. Writing brings clarity and with clarity comes peace.

UBUNTU

Ubuntu is at the center of true peace.
Ubuntu flows from traditional African Wisdom and portrays humanity at its best.
Ubuntu is about us all making it together. It implies both provision and protection.
Bishop Desmond Tutu, summarized Ubuntu by saying:

"If I diminish you, I diminish myself."

Made in the USA
Columbia, SC
18 March 2019